S

is for

Spirit Senses

Magick

Kitchen Table Magick Series

by
G. Alan Joel

Esoteric School of Shamanism & Magic

Email: *alan@shamanschool.com*
Website: *www.shamanschool.com*

Publisher: Esoteric School of Shamanism and Magic, Inc.

Disclaimer and Legal Notice:
The Esoteric School of Shamanism and Magic has made every effort to ensure, at the time of this writing, that the information contained in this book is as accurate as possible. The publisher and author make no warranties or representation with respect to the completeness, fitness, accuracy, applicability, or appropriateness of this book's contents. This book's information is provided strictly for entertainment and educational purposes. Should you choose to use or apply the ideas provided in this book, you take full responsibility for your own actions. The publisher and author provide no guarantee that your life will improve in any way should you choose to use the information presented in this book. The ability of the information provided in this book to provide self-help and life improvement to the reader is entirely dependent upon the reader. The reader's ability to gain positive results from the information presented in this book is entirely dependent on the amount of time the reader devotes to the application of the material in this book, the willingness of the reader to dedicate time and effort to learning the materials presented in this book, as well as the reader's own belief system, which may help or hinder the reader's ability to benefit from this book's materials. Since each reader differs according to willingness and openness to the information available in this book, the author and publisher cannot guarantee success or improvement for every individual reader. Neither the publisher nor the author assumes responsibility for the reader's actions, or whether the information is used for negative or positive purposes. The information contained in this book is drawn from tribal traditions—both modern and ancient—as well as the author's 30 plus years' experience researching and teaching this material to students. The information in this book is presented as interpreted by the author, and, as such, may or may not be entirely accurate. In no way should the information presented in this book be a substitute for advice from health or mental health professionals. The author and publisher are not liable—or in any way responsible—for actions

that the reader may or may not take as a result of reading the information contained in this book. The reader assumes full responsibility for his or her own actions and choices with regard to how he or she chooses to use the information in this book. The reader is strongly encouraged to choose to use the information provided in this book responsibly.

[this page intentionally left blank]

Spirit Senses Magick Blessing

Child of Wonder,
Child of Flame
Nourish Our Spirits and
Protect Our Aim.

The sense of inner silence be the first step for this magick to
be,
For the Universe whispers its answers, carried by the wind to
me.
The next step be to thank the Universe for answers and
leads,
And then to ask Universal beings to "come along" in my life
as I need.

Spirit sense magick enhances my ordinary physical abilities,
So that I can see, hear, feel, taste, touch... far more than my
usual capabilities.
With practice Spirit sense magick helps me daily,
Read people and their intentions, reliably and unfailingly.

With Water Bowls and Spiritual perimeters magick gives me
choices,
So I connect with others, Spirit-to-Spirit, when I can hear no

physical voices.
Past meanings and future situations, these I can see as well,
For Spirit senses be not limited by time or space when cast
by the correct spell!

Thus my will, so mote it be!

[this page intentionally left blank]

Free Gift

To thank you for purchasing this book, I'd like to give you a

100% FREE GIFT

Learn more about your free magickal gift.

Access Your Free Gift at
www.shamanschool.com

Find a complete list of magickal resources on https://amzn.to/3swxvPo. These resources are constantly updated so check back often!

Kitchen Table Spirit Senses Magick
Table of Contents

[this page intentionally left blank]

Introduction to Kitchen Table Spirit Senses Magick

"We're asking you to trust in the Well-being. In optimism there is magic."
~ Abraham

A Note About This Introduction

This book is one of a series of books in the Kitchen Table Magick series. Each book in the series addresses a specific area of magick (love, money, psychic development, etc.), and is written in a simple "recipe" format for people who want to use magick in their lives immediately. The Kitchen Table Magick series is akin to a Julia Childs recipe book, only these books contain magickal recipes for people to cook up some miraculous and magickal manifestations in their lives.

Because this series was designed so that each person could pick and choose to read just the books that pertain to their current life situation, each book is meant to be readable as a stand-alone book. To introduce the new reader to the series, this introduction to the series is repeated at the beginning of each book. If you have already read one or more books in this series, please feel free to jump ahead to the recipes that interest you. At the same time, some people feel that reviewing the introduction, as well as the "Rules and

1

Tips," is helpful before diving in. In magickal circles, your will is the guideline so choose whichever route best suits you... the Universe and magickal beings will follow!

What is Magick?

Many people have multiple different ideas about what magick is or can be. For the sake of clarity, here is what we know about magick after more than 35 years of study and practice. Magick is a precision science! It is also:

- The science of deliberate creation.
- The science of effective prayer.
- The science of manifesting Higher Will (substitute whatever Higher Force is most familiar to you) on the energetic and material planes.
- The science of heightened awareness, selective perception, and dynamic, harmonious relationships.
- The study of intention (as per Aleister Crowley, one of the greatest magickal practitioners in history).
- The system of creation, not coercion. Note: The word manipulation is often used in conjunction with magick, but manipulation simply means the use of the hands. It should be an "OK" word without a lot of charge, but currently it is used mostly to mean coercion. Look it up!
- The principle that every intentional act is a magickal act! Magick gives us the ability to communicate with beings on all levels, and allows us to understand, through direct experience, the actual workings of the Universe.
- The traditional path of spiritual growth.
- Not extraordinary knowledge. It is the "normal" way of life. We've just lost access to it. When you have this kind of knowledge in your understanding, you have the ability to resolve spiritual questions that otherwise become catechism. From a magickal point of view, catechism is not acceptable since a practitioner must experience and verify everything for him or herself. It

avoids the trap of dogma. In past times, having a magickal foundation was essential so that we could talk directly to higher beings in the Universal hierarchy.

- Necessary to effective religious practice.

There is some confusion as to how to spell the word "magick." There are three different commonly used spellings: magick, magic, and majick. Eliphas Levi first used the form "magick" to differentiate religious or ceremonial from stage magick. All forms of spelling are acceptable in what this author teaches.

"I love Kitchen Table Magick! It's the best mix of both mystical and down-to-earth magick I have ever encountered. The fact that I can use items from my pantry is so handy and fun! It literally is about cooking up magic at my kitchen table, and having love show up in the least expected places!"
~ Wendy J., Skokie, IL

Is Magick Real?

Yes. Magick is very real and has existed as a precise science for thousands of years. Whether you use the word magick or another name, this spiritual practice is very real. Every single person can learn to do magick. We are ALL born with the talents and abilities that empower us to do magick. The only reason that magick seems so, well, magickal is that this society no longer teaches the art and science of magick. In the distant past, magickal study was just as important as math, science, or the arts. In fact, magick was and still is the birthright of EVERY planetary citizen.

Can you learn to do the kind of magick portrayed in the movies? Yes... and no. The movies are great at giving you a taste of what you can do with magick, but they are not very accurate. In the Harry Potter movies, for instance, the characters use their Wands for every magickal operation. In reality, you can only use the Wand to handle Air energies. Your Wand would actually explode or catch fire if you tried to use it to throw Firebolts and Fireballs as the characters do in the movie.

So, what can you actually do with magick? Quite a lot. Here is a short list to get you started:

- Balance your energies for healing and manifestation
- Change old beliefs
- Defend yourself against physical and psychic attack
- Heal yourself and others
- Find hidden information and see possible futures (and change the future if you do not like the probable futures you divine)
- Psychically communicate with other beings
- Create sacred space
- Find lost people and objects
- Manifest what you want and need in life

At the very basis of magick is the understanding of the four elements: Air, Fire, Water, and Earth. Called elemental magick, these foundational elements are real. Air, Fire, Water, and Earth are part of our natural everyday environment. What makes them magickal is the understanding of how they operate not just on the physical level, but also at the levels of Mind and Spirit.

For instance, while on the physical level, Air is just the stuff we breathe. On the magickal levels Air is the conduit of psychic communication, enlightenment, understanding, dreaming, and more. If you want more of these things in your life, then you need more magickal Air. How do you get more magickal Air? Wear more Air colors, including White for communication and Sky Blue for enlightenment and understanding. To take this one step further, you could also use various magickal techniques to take on more Air to make your body lighter. Take on enough Air and you'll be able to levitate.

By just extending your understanding and use of the

basic ingredients of nature, you are doing magick! Seen in this light, magick isn't all smoke and mirrors, nor is it the result of Hollywood special effects. Magick is the result of truly understanding and working with the very elements that are all around you.

One final note: Many masters, including Wayne Dyer, have said, "You'll see it when you believe it." The same is true for magick. In other words, the suspension of disbelief and the willingness not to exercise contempt prior to investigation are requirements for magick to be "real." Magick is all around us, and always is, but our ability to perceive and use the forces of magick depends on our willingness to be open. No one else can show it to you, only your direct experience and observation can "prove" or demonstrate to you that magick is real.

[this page intentionally left blank]

What is Kitchen Table Magick?

Kitchen Table Magick is exactly what it sounds like—a series of simple recipes that you can literally "cook up" at your kitchen table using household ingredients from your own pantry and cupboard.

The Kitchen Table Magick books have been created for ordinary people who want to mix up a little magick in their lives without all the fancy rituals, but simply with everyday ingredients that can be found in the kitchen pantry, bathroom medicine cabinet, or even stuffed in the back of the junk drawer.

The goal of these books is to allow anyone with the desire to learn this craft to mix up magick literally at the kitchen table using simple recipes. What goes into a simple recipe?

- Everyday items as ingredients
- Easy to follow instructions that don't require years of training
- Procedures that take less than two hours from start to finish
- Built-in expertise that allows the magick to do the heavy lifting
- Some friendly advice on how you can help your magickal recipe provide the best results
- Oh, and a few little rules and guidelines about magickal practice in this specific arena that will keep you safe and sound, magickally speaking, when you use these recipes

Kitchen Table Magick Equals:
Quick – Effective – Safe – Everyday Use – Ordinary
Affordable Ingredients

Why Use Kitchen Table Magic?
- Everyone can do magick.
- Magick should be simple, effective, and start working right away, else it is not magick.
- Not everyone has the time or resources to enroll in a school.
- People ask us for magickal help in hundreds of emails everyday... Kitchen Table Magick is designed to help these very people.
- Of the many areas of life, most people only seem to need help in one or two areas, so you need only buy those Kitchen Table Magick books that apply to your needs.
- Magick is for the masses, and should be accessible, affordable, and simple to do. This is what our teacher taught us, and this is the legacy we are paying forward as well.
- While there are many more advanced forms of magick, these books are an introduction to that world so that you can dabble, experiment, try things out, see the result, adjust and amend, and generally have fun... just as you would cooking a meal in your kitchen.
- This book is not for the major foodie, but is perfect for the person who needs magickal help right here, right now!

Who Should Use These Recipes?
- You and anyone you know who would like a little more magick and a little less ordinary reality in their lives.
- Anyone who needs help RIGHT now and doesn't have time to fly to India or Sedona to sit at the feet of a guru.

- Anyone who does not have access to anything but a computer for help and guidance.
- Anyone who wants to do magick and then forget it (all while quietly watching the magick "do its thing").
- Anyone who wants affordable, down to earth magick they can do with regular ingredients in the comfort of home.

When to Use Kitchen Table Magic: Anytime...

- You need help.
- You don't want to do all the heavy lifting (leave that to the Angels, Spirit Guides, Animal Totems, and so forth).
- You seem stuck in a rut or corner with no way out.
- You've been struggling with a problem for a long time and need a resolution.
- You don't know what to do but you need to do SOMETHING.
- You'd like to learn how to practice the craft.
- You want to live a more magickal life and stop dealing with ordinary hassles all the time.

How Do We Know These Recipes Work?

- We teach a slew of these recipes in one-day workshops all over the country, via teleconference, and via videoconference. We also email them to people as part of our school's service work or post them on our blogs and articles library.
- We have used them for over 35 years and still do, every single day – literally tested out at our own kitchen tables for over 35 years (and at thousands of kitchen tables around the world) for a quarter century or more.
- We receive all kinds of stories and testimonials from happy successful students.

Kitchen Table Spirit Senses Magick at Work...

Read the following example to discover how Spirit senses Magick works in real life...

From Doubt to Daily Use

One of the things I love the most about Spirit senses Magick is that it starts with the frivolous and ends with the truly magickal. What I mean by this is that when I first started the Basic Magic Course (in which these skills are comprehensively taught), I was a definite 'doubting Thomas'! I did not believe that magick really worked.

I was doubly doubtful when we started the 'Come Along' exercise, in which we were to ask the Universe to 'show us' a certain unimportant item, chosen by us for this purpose. That item could be anything from chocolate to a skunk to an actor's name or a certain word.

First, I wondered if this would even work. And

then I wondered what good it would do, even if it did work. So what if I could ask and the Universe would show me a certain word during the day. Could I make money from this? Would my life be happier? How would this really help me?

I really wanted to find out, so I asked my teacher. He smiled and didn't answer my question directly. He asked me if I had developed a sufficient relationship with the Universe that my requests for 'come along' items were reliably honored. I answered that the Universe and I did indeed have a good working relationship. His smile got bigger.

He asked me to list the five biggest questions in my life, questions to which I could not get answers through normal means. He then asked me to pick one item off the list and to apply all of the Spirit sense magickal tools to the question until I received a full and satisfactory answer.

I doubted this would work, but at the time I did have a burning question about a situation in my childhood. With my teacher's help, I began the process of applying first one and then another Spirit sense magick technique until I began to get a clearer picture of the actual situation from my childhood. I have to say that not only did I get the answers I was seeking, but the process of seeking those answers transformed me from a naysayer to a big fan of magickal Spirit senses. Now I use them every day in all kinds of ways. It's super fun... and super effective!
~ Robert T., Montpelier, VT

[this page intentionally left blank]

A Few Rules and Tips About Kitchen Table Magick

As with any game, the game of life has its own set of rules. Specifically, the spiritual side of life has rules. Play by those rules and you will stay safe and easily attract what you want into your life. Break those rules and all types of unwanted consequences happen.

These "spiritual rules" are ones that have been observed, both in personal spiritual practice and spiritual practice with various associated groups and teachers. These rules universally govern any spiritual practice and appear to be in effect whether you know them or not. Unlike ethics and morals, which change with culture and time, these spiritual rules appear to have remained the same throughout time, unchanging, like physical and scientific rules.

The rules in the following section are adapted from *Rules of the Road*, as created by George Dew, co-founder of the Church of Seven Arrows. There are two major rules, which are common to most spiritual practices, along with some minor rules that are specific to our form of magickal practice.

Two Major Rules

These two rules will probably sound familiar, as they appear in most major religions and spiritual practices, most probably because they are common-sense and apply not just to spiritual practice, but to life as well.

First Rule: Golden Rule or Law of Karma
This first rule is literally a "golden oldie":

What you do to the environment or to other beings in the environment brings similar effects back to you in your life.

Often recognized as the Golden Rule or the Law of Karma, this rule tops the list because it reminds all spiritual practitioners of potential unwanted "rebound" or side effects. As your spiritual power, focus, and abilities grow, this rule will have an ever-greater impact on your life unless you exercise caution. The Universe responds more strongly and powerfully to those with focus, power, and ability.

Note: As humanity moves further in the Aquarian Age, many spiritual practitioners have seen more effects from this rule occur faster. In the past, effects of this rule that often took lifetimes to manifest now occur in minutes, days, weeks, or months. In this particular time in Earth's history, karma seems to operate under a "pay as you go" system. Simply stated, expect the effects of the Law of Karma to occur quickly.

Second Rule: The Judgment of "Good and Bad" According to the Universe
This second rule adds clarity and detail to the first rule described previously:

If you are unsure whether your acts are "good or bad"-- that is, whether those acts are in keeping with universal laws on this planet—the Universe will reflect its judgment back to you quickly, according to the "pay as you go" Law of Karma.

This law holds as true for individuals as it does for entire communities, states, nations, or other organized groups. If you are still unsure of the feedback you receive from the Universe, check areas such as your level of health,

14

the soundness of social relationships, your prosperity or lack of, sufficiency of various needs in life, and even your "luck" with appliances and machines. If your luck appears to be consistently poor, then you are probably acting contrary to universal governing laws, regardless of your intentions. The Universe cares about what you do more than what you intend.

Additional Detailed Rules

The following rules offer more detailed standards by which to measure your acts or the acts of others to determine whether these acts are in accordance with universal laws.

- Do nothing that will harm another being unless you are willing to suffer similar or greater harm. What the Universe considers "harm" may be different than what you consider harm.
- Do not bind another being unless you are willing to be similarly bound. An example of binding someone is doing acts in attempt to coerce a specific other person to love you. There is no problem with attracting your soul mate into your life, but doing acts that attempt to coerce a specific other person to love you is a type of binding.
- Never use your spiritual abilities in vain, to show off, or to boost your pride. Using your spiritual abilities from a place of pride usually causes the Universe to bring instant backlash into your life.
- If you choose to charge money or barter for using your spiritual abilities in the service of others, avoid charging extremely high prices. Charge prices for using methods comparable to other professionals, such as an attorney or accountant.
- Never use any spiritual word, chant, litany, or similar "device" unless you are confident in your understanding of its methods, intents, and effects.
- When undertaking a major spiritual operation—one that will require significant effort or attempts to create a major effect in the world—use divination to

determine whether you can safely benefit from such an operation, and to discover the obstacles you must overcome. Divination methods such as pendulum readings, channeling, meditation, and question circles (to name a few) can reveal hidden factors of which you may be unaware.

- In any spiritual endeavor, take your time, think it through, and do it right!

The good news is that you can still do Spirit senses magick rituals. The ones we teach in this book won't get you in trouble with the Universe while also allowing you to enhance your five senses and strengthen your Spirit senses and abilities.

The Ingredients of Spirit Senses Magick

"I suspect everybody has a degree of psychic ability, just as everybody has a degree of athletic or artistic ability. Some people have special gifts; other people have a particular interest that leads them to develop their abilities. But the phenomenon itself is ordinary and widespread."
~ Michael Crichton

We are all familiar with our five bodily senses of touch, taste, hearing, seeing, and smelling. What we rarely consider is our Spirit senses, how the Spirit receives information directly from the world around us, neither from body nor from mind, allowing us first-hand experience. While the body has five senses, the Spirit has over 35 that we refer to as Spirit senses or Spirit perceptics. When the Spirit has extended its perceptic apparatus into the outside world psychically, it enters the "zone" of heightened awareness and begins sending messages to body.

Correspondently, there is a similar state which body goes into as our nerve cells begin to utilize a much higher degree of their "receptors," which habitually are dormant. This we can verify by noticing such physical stimulus as "hairs standing up on the backs of our necks" or even a slight internal quivering, as though a state of excitation has been reached. Through the use of neuropeptides, the nervous system sends it messages into the brain. This can interpret the messages the Spirit is sending into a form we can recognize and use as information.

Similarly, through the Spirit senses or perceptics, shamans can gather much more information than is available to the five senses of the physical body. It takes time to develop these senses, so don't be discouraged if you don't get the results you want in the beginning. Just keep practicing the recipes in this eBook and you will refine and strengthen these Spirit senses.

Spirit Senses Magick Appetizer Recipes

Appetizers: Making Space for Spirit Sense Magick

Find Inner Silence

Come Along Game

"I've been a student of martial arts for decades and studied under many different teachers. One of the lessons that stood out the most in my history with the sport was not related to any specific technique or style. Instead, it was a comment made by one of the masters. She said, 'Adults have a more difficult time learning new skills and techniques because their minds are filled with all kinds of lists and responsibilities. Children, on the hand, have relatively large areas of free space in their minds, so they absorb and learn so much more easily than adults. Making space in your mind will lessen the learning curve for any form of martial art.' I have never forgotten this, and when I feel frustrated by lack of progress in magickal learning, I go

back and make sure I have enough sacred space in my
mind and in my life for magick to live and thrive."
~ Katharine Y., Winnipeg, Manitoba, Canada

Find Inner Silence

"Inner silence promotes clarity of mind; It makes us value the inner world; It trains us to go inside to the source of peace and inspiration when we are faced with problems and challenges."
~ Deepak Chopra

Time Required: Fifteen Minutes Per Day

One of the first things to do in awakening the Spirit senses is to get in touch with your inner silence so that you will be able to hear information the Universe sends you. This recipe gets you started on preparing your senses to receive information by engaging in a practice of meditation. If you already have a meditation program, then you are ahead of the game and can continue using your own. If you do not have one or want to just expand your program, the recipe given here can help.

Ingredients

- Comfortable place to sit
- (Optional) candle, incense, or essential oils
- At least 15 minutes of quiet, uninterrupted time

Recipe Directions

1. For at least 15 minutes, sit in a comfortable position with closed eyes, hands in your lap with right hand cradled in the left.

2. While you are aware of your thoughts, remain unattached from them. Be aware especially of your sensations.

3. If you have trouble relaxing, try lighting a candle to center your concentration, burn soothing incense, diffuse essential oils, or sit near a running fountain.

4. Now begin feeling your natural breathing as the breath moves in and out of your body. Don't force your breathing or change it any way, just feel and be aware of your body's own natural breaths.

5. As you become aware of thoughts popping up in your mind, let them pass through without focusing your attention on them. Think of this as sitting on a shoreline watching boats pass by. If you find your attention drawn to one thought in particular or find yourself hopping on that boat to explore, get off and return to shore. Simply return your focus to your breathing and let the thought pass by.

6. After at least 15 minutes of sitting in this manner you can get up and end your meditation time.

How to Use the Results of Your Recipe

There are many ways and forms that meditation can take. For the purposes of developing Spirit senses, meditation allows you to create enough quiet space and silence in your life so that you will be in a position to hear the messages sent by the Universe and from divination techniques.

Don't dwell on what happened during the meditation, or how successful you feel it was, or if you had any revelations or not. What's important is the consistency with which you do your meditation and the effort put towards doing it. Doing short meditations daily will serve you better in the long run than doing longer meditations occasionally. Consistency is a key element. Over time you will find that consistently doing this recipe will increase your ability to have inner silence and take it with you throughout everything you do. Your time spent in meditation should be an enjoyable time for you as it is time you are devoting to your inner development. The more you develop your inner life, the more benefits you will see in your outer life.

[this page intentionally left blank]

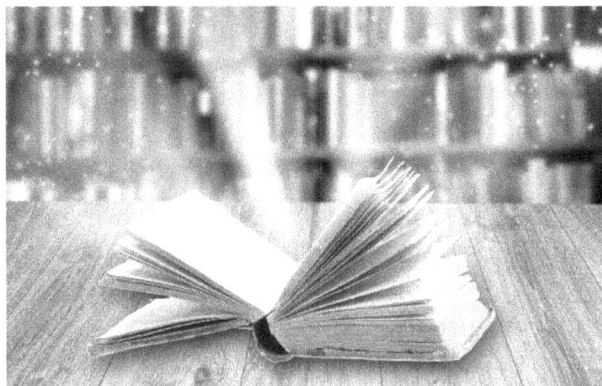

Come Along Game

"You are a living magnet. What you attract into your life is in harmony with your dominant thoughts."
~ Brian Tracy

Time Required: Ten Minutes Per Day

Establishing a relationship with higher powers and beings is important when gathering information through your Spirit senses. The more contact you have with higher powers and beings, the better your relationship is and the easier it will be to receive information from them. This recipe is a fun way to engage with the Universe and higher powers to practice communicating with them.

Ingredients
- Ideas for daily topics or books/card decks to select topics from

- Open mind and awareness of communications from the Universe

Recipe Directions

1. Once a day, make a plan to attract an event into your life. In other words, focus on something and make it "come along" into your life.

2. Choose a word, event, or topic, perhaps even a specific person - either a simple one, such as "cherries," or more complex one like the Berlin Wall or the Beatles. You could also choose a specific song that is rarely heard, such as "Wildwood Flowers" or "On Top of Old Smokey." You can even give the Universe a command such as, "Bring me cherries today."

3. You might also just turn to a page in a book or magazine, close your eyes, and point at a word or picture to select your topic, or pick a card from the Medicine cards or similar type of deck. With this type of cards, you might also want to read the meaning that goes with the card as that could be another form of communication from the Universe. Your own need and the Universe's clever forms of communication will help you select exactly what you need to hear. Whatever card, word, or image you select will be your theme for the day.

4. Now go about your day and see if that topic shows up in your life.

5. You may come across it in a newspaper, magazine, or blog article, in overhearing someone else's conversation, in a movie, on the radio or a podcast, in your internal thoughts and patterns, or a variety of other ways in the situations you encounter. Stay open to the possibilities and, as always, thank the Universe when your chosen topic shows up!

How to Use the Results of Your Recipe

The Universe is always sending us messages and has assistance waiting for us or something that we can learn. Often these messages come to us through our Spirit senses. Throughout the day, remain conscious of the message or theme you selected for the day and watch for how it applies to your interactions with others, your own internal thoughts, and situations you encounter. This simple recipe done daily helps you to operate from a place of consciousness rather than from mechanical reactions and habits, builds your relationship with the Universe and actively brings magick into your life.

[this page intentionally left blank]

Spirit Senses Magick Main Course Recipes

Main Courses: Five Senses + Spirit Senses = Pure Magick!

Stretch Your Senses

Perimeter Game

Reading People

"I have never had as much fun with magick as when we started learning how to use our Spirit senses. The best 'game' for practicing these Spirit senses was the one where we would walk into a public place and, after quieting our inner selves, begin to 'read' strangers that walked into our perceptual field. At first, I thought that I was just making things up about people because I have always had a creative imagination. But then when I would go chat with them, I would find out that a lot of my 'reading' was accurate. For instance, I could verify that a little girl's favorite color was yellow, or that the man buying a burger

had a large male dog. This fun little magickal game deepened my Spirit senses so much that I started automatically reading people wherever I went. It has saved me time, money, hassle, and more so many times since. I am so happy and grateful for this knowledge."
~ Lea R., Bar Harbor, ME

Stretch Your Senses

"If we extend our senses, we will consequently extend our knowledge."
~ Neil Harbisson

Time Required: Fifteen Minutes

Through the Spirit perceptics, shamans are able to gather much more information than is available to the five senses of the physical body. It takes time to develop these senses, so don't be discouraged if you don't get the results you want right away. Just keep practicing.

An easy way to start is to learn to expand on a sense that you are already familiar with and use, like hearing or vision. This recipe will give you directions on how to expand both hearing and vision to gather information from further away than you normally use these senses.

Ingredients
- A comfortable, quiet place to sit
- Safe place to be able to close your eyes

Recipe Directions
1. Sit in a comfortable, quiet location.

2. Close your eyes and relax (maybe do some deep breathing).

3. Draw an imaginary circle about a foot in diameter around you.

4. Listen to the sounds you hear within this circle and identify each.

5. Start with the common sounds, i.e. – children laughing, leaves rustling, someone walking by. Then move on to more obscure sounds that we usually wouldn't notice, i.e. – the wind blowing softly, an ant walking.

6. Then you can move on to widening your circle and doing the same thing.

7. See how big your circle can become. A block, five blocks, a mile?

8. Next, notice in your daily life how far out from your body your eyes tend to naturally look. Consider questions concerning your normal physical vision such as: "Do you generally look far or near?", "Do you ever look to the sides, up or down?"

9. Wherever you fail to look, begin practicing by putting your eyes there.

10. Still sitting in your comfortable location, practice

looking far out ahead of you while maintaining contact with what's right in front of you. Practice doing this and look at things further and further away.

How to Use the Results of Your Recipe

The more you practice, the more you will stop listening with your physical ears and start listening with your Spirit ears. The more you practice the physical perception of seeing, the more you will be able to see psychically or with your Spirit eyes. After practicing the above recipe, start looking for times during the day where you can apply this extended use of hearing and vision and apply this practice throughout your day.

[this page intentionally left blank]

Perimeter Game

"But magic is really only the utilization of the entire spectrum of the senses."
~ Michael Scott

Time Required: Thirty Minutes

We all have Spirit senses, but some people have more natural talent using them than others. Those without the natural talent simply need practice to develop these senses. Since we are all made up of a physical body, a mind, and a spirit, you want to by-pass sense of the mind and body to receive information from the Spirit.

The game in this recipe is a great way to get practice tuning out the five body senses and tuning in to the Spirit senses. In this game, you will shut off one of your five body senses by closing your eyes, thus cutting off access to visual data. This allows you to access or "read" the psychic or energetic information around you through your Spirit senses.

Ingredients

- Location with people where you can safely close your eyes

Recipe Directions

1. At least once a day (and obviously not while doing something such as driving) set up an energetic perimeter around yourself of about 10 – 20 feet preferably in a public place.

2. Here's the part that tells you why you don't want to be doing something like driving during this game – Close your eyes. Close your eyes and in your "mind's eye" see a circle of energy surrounding you.

3. Be aware of anytime someone enters your perimeter area.

4. When you sense that someone has entered your area, open your eyes to confirm it.

5. Once you play this game enough that you are getting accurate at sensing someone entering your area, you can increase the diameter of your circle or take another sense out of the equation. For example, you might pick a noisy area so that you don't have your sense of hearing or put on headphones or ear plugs.

How to Use the Results of Your Recipe

Remember, as we've stated in other recipes, when you start practicing to develop your Spirit senses, don't get frustrated with initial results. Learning to ignore the outcome is one of the keys to success. Over time your Spirit senses will get stronger and more accurate. In the beginning, don't worry about if your results are "right" or not.

Reading People

"We learn about people by observing their choices."
~ Claudia Gray

Time Required: Five Minutes

This recipe gives you practice using your Spirit senses to access information that you can't possibly access with your five senses. When you first start doing this recipe, don't worry about whether you are "right" or "wrong" and don't feel that you have to determine if any of your observations are correct or not. The goal of this recipe is to help you start using your Spirit senses and exercise them or practice using them. At this point you are not striving for accuracy.

Ingredients
- Pen and paper
- Watch with second hand or timer
- Public location where you can sit and observe lots of

people

Recipe Directions

1. Bring pen, paper, and a watch or timer to a very public location that has lots of people. Fast food restaurants, parks, airports, or malls are good places to start.

2. Seat yourself in a comfortable location where you can easily write, observe people, and see your timer or clock.

3. Pick a person to observe (you will need to observe them for 30 seconds). Set your timer for 30 seconds and start writing. Don't stop to think, just start writing whatever pops into your head about the person you are observing.

4. Write anything and everything that comes up about that person, whether you can directly observe it or not. It's easier to start by writing what you can observe about the person (such as hair color, clothing, activities, and so forth). While writing, don't think about what you are writing and don't allow yourself to pause to consider the accuracy or explain or validate what you have written. Don't worry about whether your observations are correct or not. Write as much as you can and as fast as you can during the 30 seconds.

5. Once the 30 seconds is up, pick another person to observe, set your timer and start writing.

6. Observe 10 people during a span of 5 minutes.

7. After you have done this recipe for a while, start consciously of expanding the type of observations you make. For example, look up and down the other person's entire body and aura. Notice things like if

their hands or feet are still or agitatedly moving. Notice if their breathing is fast, slow, shallow, or wheezing. Look at the tongue if you can and see if it is red which would mean too much Fire energy, pale and wet which could mean a deficiency or internal coldness. If the tongue is swollen and puffy with teeth marks on the edges, this would indicate a weak spleen and kidney yang. If it is stiff and wooden-like with a blunt front, this would mean they are emotionally shut down. If it is quivering with a red tip, this would indicate nervous anxiety in the neural system. Look at their eyes to see if they dart about, look at you, look through you, or move up and left or down and right. What is their posture like? Is it erect, flexible, stiff, slumped, or weak?

8. As you notice all these types of conditions, begin to build up a vocabulary of relationships between body language and inner causes and conditions. Use your own states and meanings to consider what the types of things you notice indicate. As you start training yourself to notice these types of behaviors in others and putting meanings to them, your mind will start working from your own Spirit senses and gather information from others.

How to Use the Results of Your Recipe

Here is an example of what you might write in beginning observations: "*Man, blond hair, jeans, has kids, mustache, kind, loves sports, likes water, has a brother, works outdoors, in tune with Nature, born in the West or has a connection to the West, nice tan, sneakers, talking with someone, talks with hand gestures, works well with hands, sensitive hands, sensitive nature, enjoys people, likes the color red, wears red a lot, brown eyes, around 40, likes jazz music, smiles a lot.*"

You'll notice in this short description there are many descriptors that can be seen with the five senses – the color of his hair, the way he talks with his hands, the color of his eyes, and his tan. In between, though, are descriptors that can't be seen with the five senses – that he has a brother, he is in tune with Nature, likes the color red and jazz music. These came to you through your Spirit senses. It doesn't matter if any of your descriptions, especially those that are done with Spirit senses, are actually correct. The goal is to practice accessing information with these senses. The correctness of your observations will improve with time as you practice as often as you can – any time you are waiting for a bus, sitting at a restaurant, or resting in a public setting. If you don't get out much, you can do the same exercise by turning the volume off on your TV and observing the people on your screen. The more you practice, the better your Spirit senses will get.

Spirit Senses Magick Dessert Recipes

Desserts: Magickal Water and Spiritual Flowers to Enhance Spirit Senses

Water Bowl Divination

Flower Essences

"The combination of the magickal Water Bowl and the daily use of a homemade Flower Essence to enhance Spirit senses helped me mend a relationship that had been broken for decades. Using the Water Bowl, I had to go way back in time to find one very important incident that triggered decades of misunderstanding. From there, I was able to use both Water Bowl and Flower Essences to heal the relationship on a spiritual level. From there, the relationship, as perceived through the five senses, began to right itself. Today, I would not say that the relationship has been fully restored, but without the magickal tools the relationship would have stayed permanently broken, possibly through multiple lifetimes."
~ Porter B., Richmond, KY

[this page intentionally left blank]

Water Bowl Divination

"Always remember the answers come not from the rock, the teacup, the shell, or the cards. The answers come from you."
~ Gwendolyn Womack

Time Required: Sixty Minutes

A Water Bowl is a direct form of divination that allows you to have a visual field to receive information from higher beings through your Spirit senses. It is a "bowl" formed by holding your elbows snug against your sides and lacing your fingers together in front of you into which you flow your energetic water. To safely create a Water Bowl, be sure the "bowl" does not go below your belly button and that you only use the bright blue (similar to "blue crayon" color) or what we call in magick circles, Water Blue, color of the Water element.

Ingredients
- Water Blue color source
- Place to sit comfortably
- Quiet uninterrupted time of 10 - 15 minutes

Recipe Directions
1. Have a Water Blue color source (brighter than navy blue) available as a reference.

2. Seat yourself so you can rest your elbows comfortably against your sides at or just above your hip bone points with your arms and hands extended horizontally or slightly up, angled in front of you and the tips of your fingers interlaced. This results in a "bowl" at about the level of or just above your navel. High or low bowls will have different effects. Standing, you will only affect the area above and at the level of the arms. If you do a bowl too low or are bent over, it will affect your intestinal tract, kidneys, or bladder. If you make one below the waist, it will trigger the body's mechanism for clearing water and you will go to the bathroom a lot.

3. Envision or "mock-up" a dry stream bed or ditch descending from the region of your heart into the bowl on the side nearest you. Build a spout right above the heart and allow a stream of water to flow down the ditch or stream bed into the left side of the bowl. Just see it in your mind's eye. You can also allow the water to flow out of the spout directly into the left edge of the bowl. Be sure and look at your Water Blue source as you are flowing water to be sure you are accessing the correct energetic type of Water element.

4. You can decorate the bowl on the edges if you so desire with palm trees, birds, and flowers. The Water flowing down can be a cascading mountain stream or a fountain-like stream pouring into the corner. Fill the

bowl, which should be a fairly deep bowl, until the water reaches the edge. As the bowl fills, you will likely have a sense of a rising coolness or pressure in your linked fingertips. Begin reabsorbing the water by pulling the water in your hands and up your arms from the bowl's far side. You don't need to think about this—your body knows what to do. The goal with reabsorbing the water—and re-circulating it—is to develop a smooth surface in your Water Bowl which is accomplished by smoothing out your emotions since they are Water element energies.

5. As you absorb the water energies, re-circulate the water back out to the spout so you have a continuous flow.

6. If you "see" alligators in your Water Bowl and they are dark, leave them alone. If they are healthy and you don't want them, you can blow them over the edge of the bowl.

7. As you re-circulate your water, let the turbulent feelings rush out and down the stream bed into the bowl, as with a turbulent stream down a hillside, without concerning yourself about their source. The only goal here is to smooth out the feelings so you can function in your situation at this time. To accomplish this goal, you want to have a clear top surface so continue circulating the water until you have a clear, calm surface – no waves, no rings, no bubbles, etc.

8. Once you have a calm surface on your Water Bowl, generate an emotional feeling of curiosity and focus on questions such as:
For your past: "Where was I in ..." or "What happened to me in..."
For your future: "What is likely to happen on my trip to..." or "What is likely to happen if I..."

9. Holding the focus, feeling and question, look into the Water (not through it) and wait for a picture or series of pictures to form. You may have to keep saying the question over and over until a picture forms in the Water Bowl or behind your head. As the picture starts to form, it won't cloud your Water Bowl, it will get clearer.

10. If you get a picture, but need more details or information, you can ask additional questions to clarify.

11. You can close your eyes and look at the water spiritually if you have trouble with your eyes open. You can also train your eyes to look into the Water Bowl by practicing looking at the space halfway between you and an object 20 feet away until you don't see the object, just the space.

12. In doing divinations for the future, if you are going to take a trip for instance, you can ask for a mock-up of different aspects of the trip. "What is likely to happen on my trip?" You can get a moving picture of going to the airport and getting on the plane. If you run into something that does not look OK or that is dangerous and threatening, you want to find out everything you can about that situation. Get a bigger view: the time of day, weather, the surroundings, and the events leading up to it. Then, on the trip, look for the precursor signs to appear. If they appear, change something immediately (something completely different from your plan) and you will change the outcome. A small change in the present leads to a larger change in the future.

13. When you are done, reabsorb the water by pulling all the energetic water back up into your palms and up

your arms. Failing to pull all your water energies back in may cause you to feel emotionally drained or physically dehydrated.

14. Unlace your hands. You have just completed a Water Bowl divination.

How to Use the Results of Your Recipe

The Water Bowl allows messages coming in through Spirit senses to be translated into physical information that your eyes and mind will allow. Divination tools like Water Bowls, cards and pendulums provide a conscious or physical level means for the information. Water Bowl divinations are also useful for finding lost or stolen objects or people, finding out what is happening in distant locations, exploring "forgotten" past lives and events as well as exploring future possibilities. It can also be used for other similar kinds of information such as sources of personal internal difficulties. Just change the questions you focus on and what you are curious about in Step 8. Be careful with some of these uses as you may experience powerful and unexpected emotional reactions within and from yourself. In exploring the future with any form of divination (or interpretation of dreams and visions for that matter), you need to thoroughly understand that:

- The future is not set or pre-destined. It may be changed at any time before it actually happens.
- Divinations, visions, and dreams of any particular future event are only probabilities based on an assumption that the "flows of change" currently operating will continue unchanged!
- If a divined, dreamed, or visioned future event is not what you want to happen, do some research in the Water Bowl to discover the pre-event causes and change them. If you do that, the divined, visioned, or dreamed event either will not occur at all or will occur differently than seen!

[this page intentionally left blank]

Flower Essences

"Flowers reconnect us to our own beautiful and unique essence as human beings. They wake up our positive qualities so that we feel them and they begin to emanate from us, just as each flower radiates its own unique quality."
~ Katie Hess

Time Required: Thirty Minutes

One of the best ways to receive stronger and increased guidance from the Universe and higher spiritual helpers is to increase your Spirit senses and Spirit abilities. Such senses and abilities might include clairvoyance, clairaudience, seeing possible futures, or having greater insight into current events in your life. The Universe is constantly offering us guidance and help while increasing our Spirit senses to receive these messages with greater clarity and speed. This recipe provides a variety of flower essences with descriptions of how they can help you strengthen your Spirit senses, especially when paired with other recipes in this ebook.

Ingredients
- Plants from which to make your own flower essences or flower essences you have purchased.
- Knowledge of the correct way to make flower essences if you are making your own and the materials needed to do so.

Recipe Directions
1. **Beach Plum:** Helps refine and develop the Spirit senses in addition to the five physical senses. Opens the senses to angels and higher beings.

2. **Star Tulip:** Puts us in more direct contact with Spirit guides, while at the same time developing Spirit abilities.

3. **Bayberry:** Refines and increases the ability to hear psychically, also called clairaudience. Increases the ability to hear messages from higher beings, as well as hearing the truth behind words.

4. **Caterpillar Plant:** Brings one's own inherent Spirit abilities down to a more accessible level where we can make use of them. We were born with most of these abilities, but most of them have been latent. This flower essence can call them forth for us to use.

5. **Cyclamen:** Helps one develop the Spirit ability to channel. Useful for developing spoken or written channeled messages.

6. **Jungle Flame Flower:** Particularly helpful for developing clairvoyance and integrating that Spirit ability into one's everyday senses.

7. **Lobelia:** General tonic for psychic development.

8. **Marigold:** Increases the ability to hear Spirit messages, plus the general development of Spirit abilities.

9. **Potato:** Because the potato has many eyes, the essence made from its flower helps us see on many different levels and in many different dimensions as well. Helps us understand psychic information and all the ways that information can be applied in our lives.

10. **Spikenard:** This unique essence helps extend existing Spirit abilities. The range of one's ability to hear, see, receive messages, or heal is increased when this essence is used.

11. **Sugar Bowls:** Helps open a direct connection to psychic sources, information, and use of Spirit abilities. Also allows one to access new ideas, talents, and psychic skills.

How to Use the Results of Your Recipe

By finding the essence, or combination of essences, that best suit your life, you will allow your native Spirit abilities to reveal themselves in a natural and non-traumatic way. Most of us are better at using some Spirit senses than others because these are senses that we have developed in past lives. The flower essences in this recipe simply encourage those skills to come forth into this lifetime so we can use them here and now.

[this page is intentionally left blank]

More Magickal Resources

Kindle or Paperback on Amazon:
1. *Witchcraft Spell Book Series:*
- Learn How to Do Witchcraft Rituals and Spells with Your Bare Hands (Witchcraft Spell Books, Book 1)
- Learn How to Do Witchcraft Rituals and Spells with Household Ingredients (Witchcraft Spell Books, Book 2)
- Learn How to Do Witchcraft Rituals and Spells with Magical Tools (Witchcraft Spell Books, Book 3)
- Witchcraft Spell Book: The Complete Guide of Witchcraft Rituals & Spells for Beginners (compilation of Books 1, 2, & 3)

2. *Kitchen Table Magick Series*

Ebooks and Online Courses at *www.shamanschool.com*
- Wand: Air Tool
- Athame: Fire Tool
- Chalice: Water Tool
- Plate: Earth Tool
- Magical Tool: Firebowl
- Psychic Development
- Energy Healing For Self and Others

- How to Do Voodoo
- Daily Rituals to Attract What You Want in Life

Find a complete list of magickal resources on https://amzn.to/3swxvPo. These resources are constantly updated so check back often!

Free Gift Offer

To thank you for purchasing this book, I'd like to give you a

100% FREE GIFT

Learn more about your free magickal gift.

Access Your Free Gift at www.shamanschool.com

Find a complete list of magickal resources on https://amzn.to/3swxvPo. These resources are constantly updated so check back often!

About G. Alan Joel

Magick means many things to different people. The form of magick taught by G. Alan Joel for more than 30 years is steeped in tribal traditions from around the world, from both modern tribal cultures and those from the past, which have been mostly passed on through oral dialog.

At the very heart of the magick that Mr. Joel teaches is the use of Universal Laws for the benefit of self, others, and even the planet. These magickal traditions can take on many forms, including simple rituals for daily use, specific spells for particular life situations, the use of simulacra (often better known as voodoo), weather working, water witching, the use of the elemental tools (Firebowl, Wand, Athame, Chalice, and Plate), magickal self-defense rituals, and more. Also included are the use of the Tarot for divination and spellwork, divination rituals of all kinds, Spirit-to-Spirit communication, exercises for psychic development, and abundant healing techniques.

Through his 30 plus years of studying, teaching, and honing his magickal practice, G. Alan Joel has helped thousands of people successfully integrate the magickal, and seemingly miraculous, into their daily lives. In fact, one of the greatest gifts Mr. Joel has offered through his teachings is the ability for his students to always find a magickal solution for life situations that often seem impossible to solve. With magick, anything is possible in the mundane world. All that is required of the practitioner is an open mind, the desire to learn, and a willingness to pay some time and effort into his or her magickal practice. One of Mr. Joel's favorite quotes is:

"What you pay into your practice pays you back!"

While many magickal traditions have fiercely guarded their secrets from the public, Mr. Joel feels that "Magick is the birthright of every planetary citizen." As such he strives to offer magickal teachings that are easily learned and inexpensive (no excessive fees to join exclusive magickal groups or ascend up the levels of learning). He also offers techniques that are usable and effective for all who are sincere in their desire to practice magick. In essence, Mr. Joel's methods teach a form of "Every Man's (and Woman's) Magick." All are welcome, his teachings are simple yet effective, and he also offers online classes in which he helps students troubleshoot their magickal issues in an interactive setting.

Find out more about Mr. Joel's teachings here and on his website (***www.shamanschool.com***) where magickal offerings are updated on a regular basis.

Mr. Joel augments this magickal knowledge and teaching with 30 years of practice as Doctor of Chinese Medicine, including a deep understanding of herbology and acupuncture. His understanding of the healing arts deepens the magickal knowledge he teaches, as magickal healing is a major aspect of his teachings. Mr. Joel believes that while there is clearly a time and place for Western Medicine, magickal and Eastern healing techniques can be harmoniously blended in to offer people many choices for healing all types of health conditions.

About the Esoteric School of Shamanism and Magic

The Esoteric School of Shamanism and Magic was started from a desire for all people from all over the globe to be able to attend a real, if virtual, school dedicated to magick and shamanism. The aim of the Esoteric School of Shamanism and Magic is to help people create permanent, positive change in their lives through the study of esoteric magickal and shamanic knowledge. It doesn't matter what your esoteric background is, whether you started out with witchcraft, religious studies, spirituality or candle magick, we welcome you. We believe that the Truth is the same, no matter which form you practice. We delight in all manner of shamanic schools and traditions, magickal techniques and esoteric ritual. You can visit us at *www.shamanschool.com*, our blog at *http://shamanmagic.blogspot.com*, or on social media via links on our website.

[this page intentionally left blank]

[this page intentionally left blank]

[this page intentionally left blank]

[this page intentionally left blank]